A Visit to the Ranch

By Katie Berk
Illustrated by Mike Dammer

Scott Foresman
is an imprint of

Glenview, Illinois • Boston, Massachusetts • Chandler, Arizona •
Upper Saddle River, New Jersey

Illustrations

Mike Dammer.

Photographs

Every effort has been made to secure permission and provide appropriate credit for photographic material. The publisher deeply regrets any omission and pledges to correct errors called to its attention in subsequent editions.

Unless otherwise acknowledged, all photographs are the property of Pearson Education, Inc.

12 Demetrio Carrasco/©DK Images.

ISBN 13: 978-0-328-50778-8
ISBN 10:   0-328-50778-4

18 16

Lia was excited. It was finally summer. Cousin Maria was coming to visit.

Maria had never visited the ranch before. Lia had so much to show her.

Lia loved horses and hoped that Maria would too. "Let's go riding," Lia said.

Maria looked surprised. She had never been on a horse. "Do you ride often?" she asked.

"Yes!" Lia smiled proudly. "I ride all the time."

Maria stared at the big horse. She
wanted to be brave, but she was
afraid to touch him.

"There aren't many horses where I
live," Maria said.

The girls talked about many things. Lia told Maria about the ranch.

Maria talked about life in the city. "We do lots of things," she said. "We go to museums and to the park. We ride our bikes and walk the dog in the park."

"Last summer, we went to eight baseball games. We rode on a train to get there. Our team won many games!" said Maria.

"I have never been to a real baseball game," said Lia. "And I have never been on a train."

The riders reached a stream. They decided to rest.

"You can tie the horses to this tree," said Lia's mother. "Be sure to tie good knots."

The horses drank the cool water. The girls began to wade. They laughed as they got a little wet.

"Now, I will show you the cows and the sheep," said Lia.

There was so much to show Maria. They were still riding when they saw the moon rise above them.

Maria's mother said, "I guess dinner will be a little late tonight. "

They started back to the house. They were tired and hungry.

"I am going to write to my family about life on the ranch," Maria said.

"City life sounds like fun too," said Lia.

"I have an idea," said Maria quickly. "Why don't you visit me next summer?"

"I'd love to!" said Lia.

Horses can be fun to ride, but many of them work very hard too. In New York City, some people ride in carriages. Horses pull these carriages. The carriages take people from place to place around the city and through the park.

Some farmers use horses to do work. It saves farmers money and is good for the environment. Horses are strong enough to carry logs and other heavy things. A team of horses can even do the same work as a small tractor!